D1487248

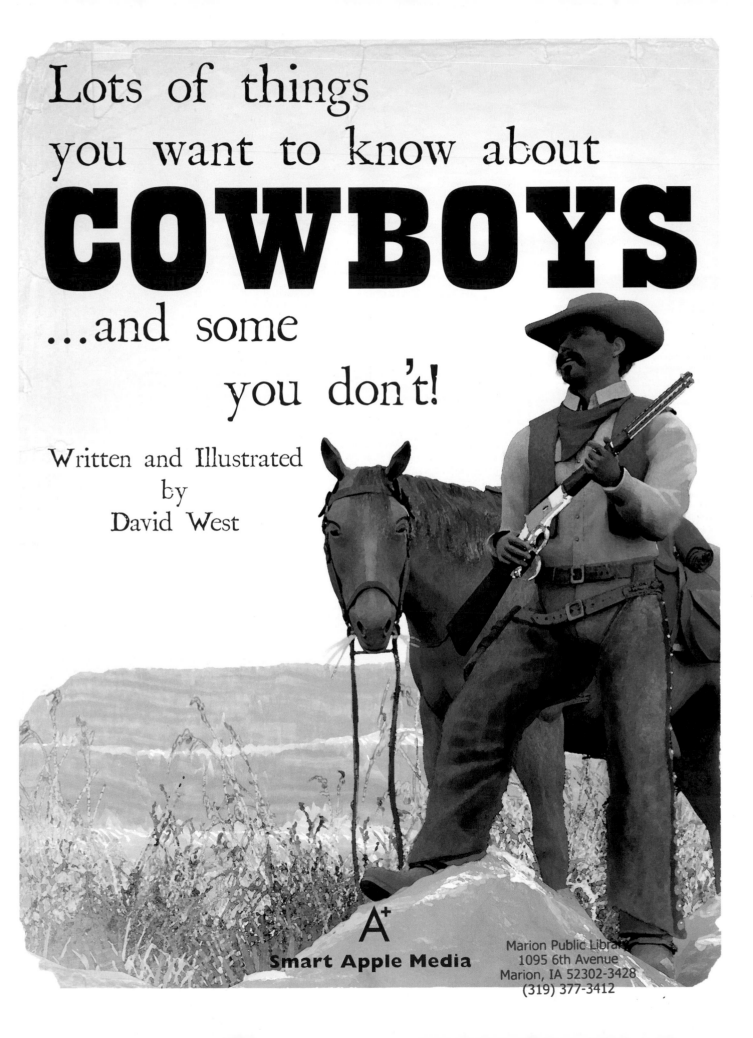

Lots of things
you want to know about
COWBOYS
...and some you don't!

Written and Illustrated
by
David West

Smart Apple Media

Published by Smart Apple Media, an imprint of Black Rabbit Books
P.O. Box 3263, Mankato, Minnesota 56002
www.smartapplemedia.com

Produced by David West ✷ Children's Books
6 Princeton Court, 55 Felsham Road, London SW15 1AZ

Designed and illustrated by David West

Copyright © 2013 David West Children's Books

Library of Congress Cataloging-in-Publication Data

West, David, 1956-
Lots of things you want to know about cowboys : ... and some you don't! / David West.
pages cm. – (Lots of things you want to know)
Includes index.
ISBN 978-1-62588-089-5
1. Cowboys–West (U.S.)–History–19th century–Juvenile literature. 2. Longhorn cattle–West (U.S.)–History–
19th century–Juvenile literature. 3. Cattle drives–West (U.S.)–History–19th century–Juvenile literature. 4.
West (U.S.)–History–1860-1890–Juvenile literature. 5. Ranch life–West (U.S.) I. Title.
F596.W484 2015
978'.02–dc23
2013030715
Printed in China
CPSIA compliance information DWCB15CP
311214

9 8 7 6 5 4 3 2 1

CONTENTS

Cowboys Wore Chaps

Cowboys out riding on the **range** for weeks on end needed clothing that was tough and durable. They wore tough cowboy boots and wide-brimmed hats to keep the sun off their heads. They also wore chaps. These were leather pant legs worn over pants as protection against thorny bushes. Chaps also helped reduce saddle sores.

Cowboys Carried Guns

Cowboys carried a pistol in a holster, mainly to use against rattlesnakes, coyotes, and other small, dangerous animals. Rifles, such as the Winchester, were sometimes carried in a saddle holster. These were useful against **predators**, such as mountain lions and grizzly bears, as well as for hunting game to add to their diet of dried meat.

Cowboys Branded Cattle with the Rancher's Mark

Different **ranchers** left their cattle to graze together on the same range, in a semi-wild state, for most of the year. Ownership of individual cattle was claimed by a distinctive brand, applied with a hot iron.

Ranchers held a roundup in the spring. Calves and unmarked older animals were branded before the herds were driven to cattle stations.

A Cowboy's Horse Is Called a Stock Horse

A typical stock horse is quite small, tough, and well-suited for working with cattle. It has a short back, sturdy legs, and strong muscles. It is intelligent and has a "cow sense." That means it understands how cattle move and will move to the right position with very little guidance from its rider.

Cowboys Herded Cattle on Long Cattle Drives

Cattle in places like Texas were driven in herds to cattle towns in Kansas, where they were put on trains to Chicago and eastern parts of the United States. An average herd of cattle might number about 3,000.

A crew of at least 10 cowboys herded the cattle. Cowboys worked in shifts to watch the cattle 24 hours a day. They drove them in the daytime and watched them at night to stop theft or a **stampede**.

The herd traveled about 15 miles (24 km) a day. They were allowed to rest and graze at midday and at night.

A Chuck Wagon Carried All the Food on a Cattle Drive

The crew on a cattle drive also included a cook, who drove a chuck wagon. He was an important member of the crew. He was in charge of cooking the food. He was also responsible for the medical supplies and had a basic knowledge of what to do if a cowboy was injured or became ill.

Wranglers Herd Horses

"Wrangler" was the name given to cowboys who caught wild horses called mustangs that roamed free on the Great Plains.

A horse wrangler on a cattle drive was in charge of the spare horses. He was often a very young cowboy who was learning to take on responsibilities.

Cowboys Tamed Wild Horses by Riding Bucking Broncos

A bronco is the name given to a wild horse. Before modern training methods, the simplest way to tame a horse was to ride it until it got used to it. Wild horses would try to throw the rider off by bucking. Bucking broncos can still be seen today at **rodeos**.

Cowboys Captured Escaping Cattle with a Lasso

Known to the cowboy as simply a "rope," the lasso was an important tool of their job. It required a special skill to twirl the loop and throw it around the head and horns of runaway cattle. The animal was then controlled from horseback and brought back to the herd unharmed.

Gauchos Are South American Cowboys

On the grasslands of South America, gauchos care for vast herds of cattle. Just like cowboys, they ride horses but, instead of lassoes, they use bolas. These are made of three weights on the ends of connected cords. Holding one of the weights, the gaucho swings the other two above his head and throws the bola to entangle the legs of cattle.

A Cowboy in Australia Is Called a Stockman

Stockmen, also known as "ringers" in some parts of Australia, work on ranches called stations. They often use working cattle dogs called koolies to help round up the cattle.

Cattle Can Stampede

Cattle can become very nervous, especially at night. A lightning strike or horse shaking itself can trigger a stampede. Cowboys attempt to turn the stampeding herd into itself by riding in front and firing their pistols. The loud bangs make the leaders of the stampede turn so that the herd ends up running in a circle before eventually calming down.

Cowboys Ate Lots of Beans

Cowboys on the trail ate dried meat, sometimes boiled in water to make a broth. A rare treat was fresh meat from hunting. Hard cheese was often included in the rations and was normally added to chili beans or cooked in biscuits using a **Dutch oven**. But beans made up the bulk of a cowboy's diet, along with a plentiful supply of coffee and some dried fruit.

Cowboys Were Paid at the End of the Trail

At the end of the trail was the cattle town. After months of hard work and dull food, cowboys were paid off and turned loose. They bathed and shaved, bought new clothes, and partied in the town's many **saloons**.

Cowboys Got into Gunfights

Cattle towns attracted a very rough crowd and with them came violence. Bill Bailey, a Texas cowboy, was gunned down outside a saloon in the cattle town of Newton. When his cowboy friends heard about it, they vowed to take revenge against his killer. In the gunfight that followed seven men were killed in what is famously known as the "Newton Massacre."

You Can See Cowboys and Cowgirls at Rodeos

Cowboys still work today on ranches around the world. The best place to see cowboys and cowgirls, though, is at a rodeo. You can see them in action, racing horses around barrels, lassoing and tying down calves, wrestling steers, riding bucking broncos, and even riding bulls.

Rodeo Clowns Have to Be Quite Brave

Bull riding can be very dangerous. The bull is likely to step on its fallen rider. Rodeo clowns distract the bulls and help prevent injury to competitors.

Cowgirls Worked on Ranches

When men went to war or on long cattle drives, women often took over the work of a cowboy on the ranch. There were even a few cases of cowgirls working on cattle drives. It wasn't until the **Wild West Shows** arrived that cowgirls became famous. Cowgirls can still be seen today at rodeos.

Glossary

Dutch oven an iron cooking pot with a tight-fitting lid

predators animals that hunt other animals for food

ranchers people who own ranches where cattle or sheep are raised

range a large area of grazing land without fences or other barriers

rodeos sporting events that test the skills of cowboys and cowgirls in a number of sports which involve horses and cattle

saloons a bar of the Old West that provided beer, liquor, food, and lodging

stampede when a herd panics and begins running with no clear direction or purpose

Wild West Show a traveling performance filled with cowboys, Native Americans, wild animals, outlaws, buffalo hunts, and bucking broncos

Index